No Treat for the Seal!

By Sally Cowan

On the weekend,
Lee went out on the sea
with Dad.

Chief Kealy greeted them.
She would drive the boat.

"It's time to leave!"
called Chief Kealy.

Beep! Beep!

The boat made a stop
by a sandy beach.

"You can swim at this spot!"
said Chief Kealy.
"It's not deep!"

I just see lots of green seaweed!

I can see a red crab creeping by.
It's next to your feet!

Chief Kealy wheeled out some lunch on a trolley.

Lee could see a seal in the sea.

"That cheeky seal can smell the meal!" said Lee.

"Shall we feed it a treat?" said Dad.

"We should not give
the seal a treat!" Lee said.
"Seals need to hunt
for each meal."

"He can go and feast on
some fish, then!" said Dad.

On the trip back,
Chief Kealy let Lee help
with the boat's big wheel.

The boat got back to the dock.

Dad said, "Is it okay if **we** eat a treat, please, Lee?"

"Yes!" said Lee. "**We** can eat a treat!"

CHECKING FOR MEANING

1. Who was in charge of the boat? *(Literal)*
2. What did Dad see in the sea? *(Literal)*
3. Why do you think Lee said that seals should hunt food for themselves? *(Inferential)*

EXTENDING VOCABULARY

seaweed	What are the two smaller words that make up the word *seaweed*? How do these words help you understand the meaning of *seaweed*? What does seaweed feel like?
trolley	Say the word *trolley*. How many sounds are in the word? Which letter or letters make each sound? Where else might you find a trolley?
cheeky	What does it mean to be cheeky? Why do you think the author described the seal as cheeky?

MOVING BEYOND THE TEXT

1. What did you learn about seals from the story? What else do you want to know?

2. What is your favourite activity to do with family or friends?

3. Have you ever seen a boat in real life? Was it a small boat or a big boat? Where was the boat? What did you notice about it? Would you like to ride in a boat?

4. Lee and Dad saw seaweed, crabs and a seal. What else might you see near or in the ocean?

TIME TO WRITE

Write about what you might see on a boat trip.

PRACTICE WORDS